C000114554

River Mersey
Gateway to the World

Trinity Mirror Media

Editor: Peter Elson
Design & Production: Vicky Andrews
Cover Design: Lee Ashun
Liverpool Daily Post & Echo Image Archive:
Brian Johnston

Pictures copyright Liverpool Daily Post & Echo
unless otherwise stated

Business Development Executive Editor: Ken Rogers
Senior Editor: Steve Hanrahan
Editor: Paul Dove
Senior Art Editor: Rick Cooke
Trinity Mirror Media Marketing Executive: Claire Brown
Sales and Marketing Manager: Elizabeth Morgan
Sales and Marketing Assistant: Karen Cadman

© 2012 Trinity Mirror/Liverpool Daily Post & Echo

All Rights Reserved. No part of "Gateway to the World" may be
reproduced, stored in a retrieval system, or transmitted in any form,
or by any means, electronic, mechanical, photocopying, recording or
otherwise without the prior permission in writing of the copyright
holders, nor be otherwise circulated in any form of binding or
cover other than in which it is published and without a similar
condition being imposed on the subsequent publisher.

Printed by PCP

ISBN 9781908695031

To buy prints of the images in this publication,
or any photos in our archive collection,
visit www.merseyshop.com/buyaphoto
or telephone 0845 300 3021

FORTY YEARS ON . . .

Turn left for New Brighton — or right for New York. Are you taking the Royal Iris for the Wirral, or the Anchor Line across the Atlantic?

THE photograph to the left, taken on June 15, 1963, speaks not only a thousand words, but also stands for many thousands of voyages and millions of passengers who passed over the Liverpool landing stages.

Some sailings were local and others long enough to reach the far ends of the earth, but they all started here.

The landing stages were the focal point for the countless souls who beat a pathway to Liverpool, once the world's greatest mercantile city.

Over the centuries, in that lost world before air travel, Liverpool was a legendary place of departure and arrival that grew and grew in importance.

It reached its apogee with the Princes Landing Stage and George's Landing Stage, which were the point of it all: a sort of half-way floating house, betwixt solid land and movable ships.

Although technically two stages, with George's Stage for the Mersey ferries and Princes Stage for the liners and Isle of Man traffic, they were seamlessly joined together. In tandem, measuring a quarter of a mile in length, they formed the longest floating structure on earth.

For the Mersey ferry commuters, the stages were just one part of a trip to the office and on the way back home in time for tea.

Yet for other travellers, in a period stretching over almost a century, this combined landing stage was the first or last part of Great Britain on which they trod, in peace and wartime, by choice or towards their doom.

They were served by shipping lines whose names were international brand names: Anchor, Bibby, Blue Funnel, Blue Star, Booth, British India, Canadian Pacific, Cunard, Elder Dempster, Furness Withy, Lamport & Holt, Pacific Steam Navigation, Shaw Savill and White Star.

But by late 1972 with the last liner traffic gone, this marvellously eccentric floating village with its myriad of jobs and workers was facing its own demise: uneconomic, old and obsolete, once a place of so much heightened emotion, its only friend now was the scrap man.

Yet for all its creaking pontoons and joints (and they really did creak), undulating in the swell, it served faultlessly for a century until demolition in 1974. ➤

ALL ABOARD

School children and teachers pack the rails of SS Nevasa as they set off from Princes Landing Stage for a western Mediterranean educational cruise in October, 1966.

➤ That's more than can be said for its successors, whose only claim to fame was that they both sank.

However, now we're in the latest and a more serious era, with a greater commitment to making this new, fourth waterfront landing stage complex work.

It is exactly 40 years since the ocean liners, m/v Aureol and ss Uganda, departed the Princes Landing Stage on their last round voyages.

Many people aware of this depressing fact could never imagine that history would repeat itself. But well into the jet age, once again "turnaround" voyages (ie starting and ending here) will restart in May, 2012.

This is when Cruise & Maritime Voyages' m/v Ocean Countess will inaugurate the first of 12 cruises this summer from the new Liverpool Cruise Terminal, which sits in the place of the old Princes Landing Stage.

It's only a small beginning, but with Fred Olsen Cruise Lines' m/v Boudicca restarting her 2013 Liverpool cruise programme from the Cruise Terminal, the sky – or should I say sea – will be the limit.

Just as people used to flock to Liverpool because it was the best place to get on a ship to the four corners of the earth, so they will do again. If Liverpool is the gateway to the world, the landing stage was, and will become again, the doorstep.

As The Carpenters sang, "This is only just the beginning. . ."

Peter Elson

WHITE EMPRESS

Below, surely the most beautiful ocean liner to grace the Mersey, Canadian Pacific's three-funnelled Empress of Scotland, approaches the landing stage in the mid-1950s, as the beleaguered Green Goddess trams cling on to their Pier Head turning circles.

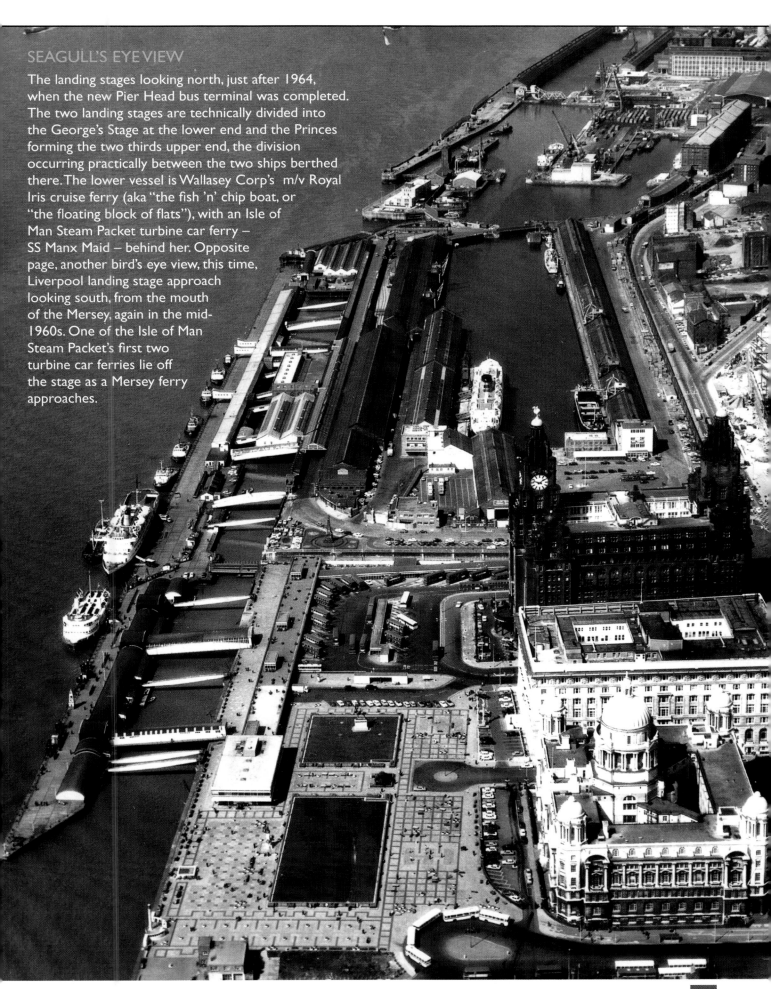

SEAGULL'S EYE VIEW

The landing stages looking north, just after 1964, when the new Pier Head bus terminal was completed. The two landing stages are technically divided into the George's Stage at the lower end and the Princes forming the two thirds upper end, the division occurring practically between the two ships berthed there. The lower vessel is Wallasey Corp's m/v Royal Iris cruise ferry (aka "the fish 'n' chip boat, or "the floating block of flats"), with an Isle of Man Steam Packet turbine car ferry – SS Manx Maid – behind her. Opposite page, another bird's eye view, this time, Liverpool landing stage approach looking south, from the mouth of the Mersey, again in the mid-1960s. One of the Isle of Man Steam Packet's first two turbine car ferries lie off the stage as a Mersey ferry approaches.

PANORAMIC

The best view of the Liverpool landing stages was on the river or from the Wirral shore. From the vantage point of the Seacombe Landing Stage on June 25, 1960, are the coastal minesweeper, HMS Mersey, front left, and Wallasey Corp ferry St Hilary (ex-Royal Daffodil). Across the river at Princes Landing Stage is Canadian Pacific's Empress of France (II), back right, in her last season of service, complete with her new trendily tapered cowel-topped funnels, so the grand old dame did not lose face alongside CP's new postwar "white empresses". The prow of Isle of Man Steam Packet's Ben-My-Chree (built by Cammell Laird in 1927) can be seen back left.

> " The Mersey was the main transport artery for home and abroad. "

MERSEY GATEWAY

These late Victorian views show the landing stages in their early years when the Mersey was the main transport artery for home and abroad. The colour-tinted postcard (courtesy of Stephen Guy) shows Cunard Line's Blue-Riband winner, RMS Lucania, built in 1893.

RAIL AND SAIL

Princes Landing Stage c1896, with White Star Line's famous tug tender Magnetic, steaming off, centre right, with an early White Star liner behind her, combining sail and steam. Liverpool Riverside station, opened in 1874, brought liners to the landing stage, which had previously served only Irish and Manx vessels. At this date the stage itself is still bare of structures and the tallest landside buildings are Albert Dock's warehouses, top centre left.

BUSTLING

Horse drawn vehicles on the stage, c1912, including one on the floating roadway belonging to Cheshire Lines at Central Station. Two Wallasey luggage boats are moored, left, in this pre-Mersey Tunnel era, and a Bibby liner is docked, right.

SITTING PRETTY

The test beds for Cunard Line's new generation of turbine liners were its "pretty sisters" of 1905, Carmania and Caronia. One of which, probably RMS Carmania (I), is at Princes Landing Stage, in July 1927, with her derricks lifting the last freight aboard, but with steam up and ready for the off. She is dressed overall as is a Bibby liner, behind, most likely SS Cheshire on her maiden voyage. Note the well-dressed couple, front centre left, you can almost hear the rustle of her ladyship's furs down the years.

HERE'S LUCY

Lusitania alongside Princes Landing Stage attended by Cunard's tug tender Skirmisher and the paddle steamer Reaper, with Riverside station behind. Liverpool's position as the second city of empire was reinfornced by the Cunard superliner sisters, RMS Lusitania and RMS Mauretania (I), in 1907, then the world's biggest ships. Lusitania's sinking on May 15, 1915, after being torpedoed by U-20 causing the deaths of 123 US passengers, was a factor in bringing the US into the First World War. Out of 1,958 people onboard, 1,198 perished

FORCEFUL

The magnificent spectacle of RMS Lusitania in the river is enjoyed by crowds on the landing stage and aboard the Alexandra Towing Co's tug tender paddle steamer, probably for George King V's visit in July, 1913, to Merseyside.

"At the turn of the 20th century, Lusitania and Mauretania were the world's biggest ships."

AUTUMN CLOUDS

Smoke belches from SS Mona's Isle's funnels, right, as she embarks passengers for a late holiday season weekend in the Isle of Man, on October 3, 1938. Behind her, the Cunard liner Lancastria returns from a cruise. Moored ahead of Mona's Isle at the stage is Mersey Docks' pilot boat No 3 James H Beazley and further along Alexandra Towing's tug tender, either Flying Breeze or Egerton. Mona's Isle's radio officer was Harold Bride, the only surviving radio officer from RMS Titanic. Less than a year later the Second World War was declared and Lancastria was bombed and sunk at St Nazaire, on June 17, 1940, with at least 4,000 people killed – the worst UK maritime loss of life ever.

"It was a big day of celebration when 'The Maury' set sail for her maiden voyage to New York in 1939."

PUT OUT THE FLAGS

It was a big day of celebration – albeit a wet one – when Cunard's brand new RMS Mauretania (II), built by Cammell Laird at Birkenhead, set sail for her maiden voyage to New York on June 17, 1939. "The Maury" was the largest ship built in England, as the biggest liners tended to be constructed on the Clyde or at Belfast. Huge crowds and even an obligatory traffic jam greet the 35,000 gross ton liner arriving at the stage to load passengers. Note the Titanic Memorial, bottom left of the picture.

PUT OUT MORE FLAGS

Led by tug tender Flying Breeze, RMS Mauretania arrives at Princes Landing
Stage, on April 24, 1947, to prepare for her second maiden voyage, after
postwar reconversion from troopship back to luxury transatlantic liner.
The old lightvessel Wreck marks the sunken Ullapool, while Riverside Station
has been reduced to a shell during the Blitz. The destroyer HMS Crispin,
already alongside the stage, had brought the Duchess of Kent from Belfast.

FULL ASTERN!

Trying to negotiate the
wartime wreck of the
Ullapool and its marker
ship (seen marked mid-
river on above photo),
Maury's second maiden
voyage got off to a rivet-
brushing start with Blue
Funnel's Memnon leaving
Alfred Lock. A collision was
averted – just – but the
belching smoke says it all.

EASTER PARADE

Cunard's RMS Carinthia makes a very rewarding sight for visitors on stage during Easter weekend, March 29, 1959, to see "if there's anything interesting in". The Cunarder has just disembarked passengers from New York is and heading down river to unload cargo in Huskisson Dock.

DRESSED OVERALL

Flags flying for her last round trip to Bombay, Anchor Line's Circassia loads passengers and this Vauxhall car at Princes Landing Stage, on March 14, 1966.

ROYAL RETURN

Left, Pacific Steam Navigation Co's final ocean liner flourish, or "act of faith", was the 1956 flagship Reina Del Mar – Queen of the Sea. After only eight years on the Liverpool – South America Pacific coast run, jet planes had stolen her passengers and she was rebuilt as a cruise liner. Leased to Travel Savings Assocation for cut-price cruising, she is seen coming alongside the Pier Head in 1964. Picture: Ian Collard.

HOMECOMING

The Princes Landing Stage master's crew, in their dock board regulation issue of caps and oilskins, struggle in a gale to secure a camel barge (used as a spacer to keep moored ships in deeper water) on November 28, 1967. With no pilot or Royal Mail flags, Cunard's cruise liner RMS Franconia must have just arrived, prior to a refit and rare Christmas cruise from the Mersey (she was usually US-based). Built as Ivernia in 1954 for the Canadian liner service, her 1963 £6m rebuild for cruising cost 50% more than her original £4m construction!

NICK OF TIME

Captain Nick Nash, on the bridge of his command, Princess Cruises' megaliner Crown Princess, on the very berth where, as a youngster in the 1960s, he sailed on Elder Dempster's Accra and Apapa, on visits to his father, an engineer working in West Africa. Capt Nash, whose family comes from Cornwall, said: "We used to travel on the night sleeper from Penzance to Liverpool Lime Street and get on the ship the next day." Crown Princess, at 113,000 gross tons, is more than ten times the size of Accra or Apapa, which were 11,600 grt.

EASTERN PROMISE

Apapa is shown arriving at the stage for her last and 177th round voyage to West Africa, in September 21, 1968. She was sold to Shun Cheong Steam Navigation Co, who renamed her Taipooshan for service in the Far East.

WEST AFRICA BOUND

Scudding clouds dapple Elder Dempster Line's flagship, the lovely m/v Aureol in light and shade, as her derricks move cargo during her Liverpool turnaround, on October 12, 1956. Aureol was the last ocean liner based in Liverpool and was relocated to Southampton in 1972 when the Princes Landing Stage was declared too costly to maintain for her visits every six weeks.

BOAT DRILL

A light summer breeze ripples the Mersey on August 11, 1966, as photographer Stephen Shakeshaft catches Canadian Pacific flagship Empress of Canada (III) practising life-boat drill in mid-river. In front is the new Pier Head bus station, as a Wallasey Corp ferry (either Leasowe or Egremont) approaches George's Stage, right, and a Manx turbine steamer pokes her bow in, far right.

IMPERIAL ELEGANCE

Showing off the elegant sheer to her hull, Canadian Pacific's SS Empress of England arrives at the stage to load passengers for her Christmas cruise to Lisbon, Dakar, Las Palmas and Madeira, on December 20, 1968. She sports the company's new livery, which replaced the much-loved buff funnel with its red and white chequer-board logo. The midship's legend CP Ships was soon removed after some waggish painter altered it to "Cut Price Ships" just prior to CP directors viewing the new look at Montreal!

BOAT DRILL II

Canadian Pacific's Empress of England gets her lifeboats checked at Princes Stage, as m/v Royal Iris sails past for New Brighton on a summer day in the mid-1960s.

TRANSATLANTIC

Holland America Line's flagship, m/v Rotterdam, 61,849 gross tons, carrying 1,404 passengers, made her maiden arrival in Liverpool from New York, on May 26, 2009 – the first time in 43 years a liner had sailed this pioneering route.

CHECKING IN

It must be 1964 as the women's Mary Tyler Moore-style hair-dos almost perfectly date this scene at Princes Stage customs check-in. New York-bound passengers have just disembarked from the London boat train at Riverside station and wait with their baggage to board Sylvania on July 23, 1964.

SEEKING CLOSURE

Liverpool's New York service ended when Cunard Line's RMS Sylvania made the final return trip in November, 1966, as seen here at the same berth as Rotterdam more than four decades earlier.

KEY STAGE LEARNING

When that great artery of Empire, the British India Steam Navigation Co found itself with a fleet of redundant troop ships in the early 1960s, it hit on a wizard wheeze. Mass army travel had migrated to air in 1962, but there were other large numbers of undemanding, regimented potential passengers at hand, willing to fill the shipboard dormitories – school children. So BI greatly expanded its sporadic educational cruises, running many of them from Liverpool. Forty years on there will be a generation to whom the names Devonia, Dunera, Dilwara, Nevasa and Uganda will bring back warm memories of youthful cruises around Europe and their first trips abroad.

Pictured left, Moreton Secondary Modern school girls attend their muster station aboard SS Uganda, with ship's matron, Miss Diana Branch, at the start of an educational cruise to Corunna, Gibraltar, Tangier and Lisbon, on October 18, 1968, carrying 850 pupils and 16 teachers, from Wirral, Chester and north Liverpool.

THE 'UG TUG'

SS Uganda, seen at Princes Stage on August 2, 1972, performed the last turnaround voyages from Liverpool in that month. Uganda had been displaced from the UK – East Africa liner run and this slim 14,430 gross ton colonial lady became a rather dumpy–looking 16,607 gross ton hausfrau after conversion at Hamburg for educational cruising. The schools' cruises ended when Uganda was requisitioned as a hospital ship for the Falklands War in 1982.

STRUCK OFF

Shore riggers broke their unofficial support of the national dock strike on August 2, 1972, to moor SS Uganda at Princes Landing Stage and unload luggage. The liner had arrived with 671 school children after an educational cruise to Iceland and Norway. The youngsters look uneasy about their cases' fate as does the junior officer, centre, about his future UK merchant naval career prospects (or lack of them) – but dig those classic early '70s sideburns.

> **"The names Devonia, Dunera, Dilwara, Nevasa and Uganda will bring back warm memories of youthful cruises."**

THEY'RE OFF!

Youngsters crowd SS Nevasa's rails in fine spring weather as 1,000 pupils leave Liverpool on April 28, 1966. Nevasa, 20,746 gross tons, was chartered by Liverpool, Bootle and Birkenhead education authorities for the cruise to Madeira, Casablanca, Gibraltar and Lisbon. Built in 1956 as British India Line's centenary ship, Nevasa carried 187,000 students on 200 voyages before she was scrapped in 1974, when the oil crisis made her too costly to run.

SHAKE A LEG

School girls put their best foot forward before boarding SS Nevasa on Princes Landing Stage.

LOUD REPORT

Plenty of laughter from youngsters aboard m/v Devonia, 12,795 gross tons, as she pulls away from Princes Landing Stage on October 20, 1967, as they shout farewells to their parents. Reports were sent back to the Liverpool Daily Post by 11 of the pupils on the cruise to the western Mediterranean and North Africa.

MUSIC OF THE NIGHT

It's cold and dark, but Liverpool Youth Orchestra conducted by Stanley Gill put on a fine show of musicianship and woolly hats to send off British India's m/v Devonia, on her final voyage from Liverpool, on November 5, 1967.

SUBTLE LINK

Moored ahead of BI's SS Nevasa, on September 15, 1969, is the Isle of Man Steam Packet's gorgeous SS Lady of Mann, built in 1930, as its centenary ship. Looking deserted at the end of a busy day criss-crossing the Irish Sea, the Lady only has two years' service to go, but still looks in great fettle.

PROGRESS

Steam turbine speedsters like Lady of Mann have long gone in favour of light-weight, high speed catamarans such as SuperSeaCat Two, passing the remains of the stage in January, 2007, where Lady of Mann and Nevasa were tied up nearly 40 years earlier.

EXODUS

Hundreds of motorcyclists started their annual pilgrimage to the Isle of Man for the annual TT Races. Queues were lengthy but every one got away for this first day on May 29, 1988.

WHEELY GOOD

Ten years earlier, motorcyclists were packing onto the landing stage as the Steam Packet ferries just about coped with the rush with a continuous shuttle service to Douglas. Here they pour onto m/v Mona's Queen, on June 2, 1978. SS Manxman lies behind.

BON VOYAGE

Well-wishers witness the crowded first sailing of the brand new
Liverpool & North Wales SS Co's flagship St Tudno, built to replace
paddle steamer La Marguerite. As St Tudno wheels away from the
stage on her maiden voyage to Llandudno and Menai Bridge, in
1926, lurking behind her bow is our old friend, the White Star Line
tender SS Magnetic.

STAGE BOUND

Looking over the foredeck of a North Wales steamer, probably St Seiriol, the
fire boat William Gregson is on station at the tip of George's Stage. Famously,
she never squirted a hose at a real fire and was in dry-dock when the "big
one" occurred – Empress of Canada's destruction in Gladstone Dock, in 1953.

LOVELY DAY OUT TO BANGOR

A fabulous photo of just another day on the North Wales run, as the great paddle steamer La Marguerite loads at the landing stage, as the destination board says, for: "Llandudno, Beaumaris, Bangor and Menai Bridge. Leave 10.45am due back 7.30pm." La Marguerite was withdrawn in late 1925, so this view dates from the early 1920s, as we can see by the ladies' cloche hats. Picture: F.A. Fyfe

BUSY BUSY

It's hard to imagine now what a thriving, crowded place the Liverpool landing stages once were – and here's the hard evidence. Putting that valuable British characteristic of queuing into good practice, thousands of holiday makers patiently wait for the Isle of Man boats on the morning of July 28, 1956. The queue starts as far as the eye can see on the approach to the Pier Head (centre right), snakes along the far side of Riverside station (top) and winds up and down both platforms inside (centre left). Six years later, pictured below, and the morning queue runs (well, stands) along Princes Parade, beside Riverside station. We assume it's not been the same people waiting six years to board.

SITTING ROOM

Top, Isle of Man-bound passengers reached
the big waiting room, here on May 30, 1959. At
these peak times, the entire Steam Packet fleet
of seven ships would be running a continuous
shuttle service round the clock to Douglas.

ALMOST THERE

SS Manxman on the morning of July 2, 1966, is
the first ship away after the six week seamen's
strike – so the passengers will be delighted that
their holidays will go ahead. Behind is the brand
new IoMSPCo car ferry SS Ben-My-Chree.

STRIKE UP THE BAND

Main picture, aircraft carrier HMS Centaur's Royal Marines Band play to crowds on the stage and flight deck on Sunday evening, August 15, 1965, on a Home Fleet Squadron visit for Liverpool Navy Week (yes, we actually had those).

TOWERING ABOVE

Framed by the towers of Our Lady & St Nicholas, Liverpool seamen's church, and the Royal Liver Building, seafarer Elizabeth Dawson stands on HMS Illustrious' flight deck in 2009

"Although Liverpool was never a Royal Navy base, it was regarded very highly by the Senior Service."

SEA POWER

The new mighty Ark Royal (IV) makes another foray on her
trials from Cammell Laird shipyard, Birkenhead, watched by
an appreciative crowd on the landing stage, on May 2, 1954.
This Audacious class aircraft carrier was the world's first
commissioned example with an angled flight deck.

FLYING IN

Light aircraft carrier HMS Centaur's De Havilland Sea Vixen Mk Is are lined up on the flight deck with the Royal Liver Building clock towers behind – January, 1963.

FLOWN AWAY

Two units of Britain's now scrapped Sea Harrier fleet on display in the same spot, more than 40 years later, on carrier HMS Illustrious.

HOMECOMING

Merseysiders turn out for a return visit by HMS Ark Royal (IV), 43,060 gross tons, to her birthplace on June 28, 1970. She was withdrawn and scrapped in 1979.

LAST CALL

The final visit to Liverpool of light aircraft carrier HMS Ark Royal (V), 22,000 grosss tons, of 1985, to the city before decommissioning in 2011, is marked by a display from one of her Sea King helicopters.

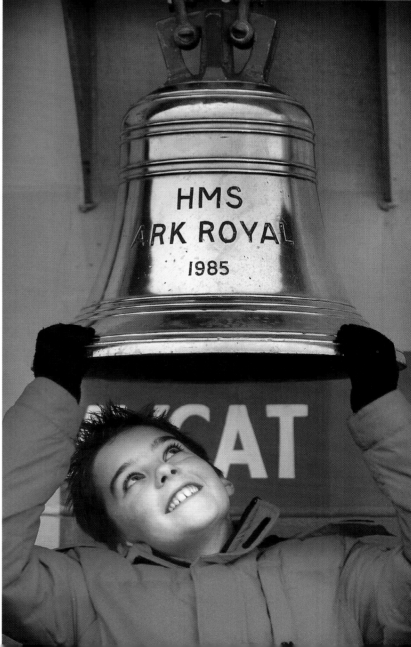

REVEALED

Top right, the famous wartime carrier Ark Royal (III), 28,160 gross tons, passes George's Stage and the Pier Head trams as she sets off from her builder, Cammell Laird, Birkenhead, for trials in Liverpool Bay, late in 1938. After a very active but short war, she was torpedoed and sunk on November 14, 1941.

RINGING THE CHANGES

Right, Luke Barber, aged 11, from Bebington, with Ark Royal's bell in 2009 – in an unrepeatable photo as the ship is now decommissioned.

HOAX CALL

If you thought the threat of bomb threats and disruption to innocent travellers started in the 1970s, think again as Liverpool was ahead of the game. In a bizarre event, the IoMSPCo's Lady of Mann received a message claiming there was a bomb aboard after departure for Douglas from Princes Landing Stage, on August 2, 1961. The venerable old girl performed an emergency U-turn at the Mersey Bar and raced back to the stage. Passengers were told there was a mechanical fault. The ship was safely docked (left) and searched to no avail. Senior police and officials discuss the hoax as disgruntled passengers receive their refunds.

PADDLING IN

Making a welcome visit in April, 1977, the preserved Clyde paddle steamer Waverley approaches the landing stage. This was the first time a paddler had been to the landing stage since the 1930s. Waverley returned in 2001, but in spite of pleas, her current managers have not been tempted to come back since then.

GRAB THIS

The stage has also hosted other unusual vessels, such as Mersey Docks & Harbour Board's new steam grab dredger No 24, seen going astern prior to trials in 1937.

GLAD TO BE HERE

Women of the India and Burma Services who took part the May, 1946 Victory March, in London, pictured on the Cunard troopship Mauretania, on May 22, 1946, alongside Princes Stage.

DESPERATE TO GO

Some of the 300 Canadian troops who walked off Canadian Pacific's troopship Empress of Scotland at Princes Stage, in protest over allegedly poor conditions, on December 10, 1946. By this time after the war, there was plenty of unrest among Allied soldiers who just wanted to get home.

ALL SO ROSY DEAR

Send chicken soup down to the Pier (Head): Barbra Streisand touches up her red lead and barnacle remover as she prepares to film Yentl on the Isle of Man Steam Packet's SS Manxman, at Princes Stage, on September 23, 1982.

DOCTOR GO

Actor James Robertson Justice, famous for playing curmudgeonly Sir Lancelot Spratt in the "Doctor" comedy films, beams at a press in call in his suite on Cunard's RMS Media, before sailing for New York on October 30, 1955, en route to film in Mexico.

SEA SHANTY

Royal Iris hosts the Liverpool Philharmonic Choir's river charter from the Pier Head on July 5, 1976.

AVAST YE!

Liverpool DJ Billy Butler sports a seaweed style perm as he skippers the Mersey Pirate (alias m/v Royal Iris) for an ITV children's morning show in June, 1979.

GOING LOOPY 1

Landing stage seaman Tommy McDonogh makes fast the bow rope of pilot boat No 2 Edmund Gardner, in June 1961. This vessel is preserved at Canning Dock, by Mersey Maritime Museum.

GOING LOOPY II

"Come in, Empress of Canada, your time's up."
Princes Stage switchboard operator Edward
Roberts, of Seaforth, makes some connections
in June 1961, dealing with radio ship to shore
requests for berths and other instructions.

DEEP THOUGHT

Two generations soak up the atmosphere as tug Holmcock
pulls away (note the cockerel silhouette on the mast top).
New Brighton Tower Ballroom is on the horizon, right.

DOWN THE HATCH

Inspecting the landing stage pontoons, in June 1961, with a trusty oil
lamp are, from left, Mr E Parr, Mr W Ellis and foreman Mr J Giles.

IN MEMORIAM

The Royal Marines Forces Volunteers are inspected during the annual Zeebrugge raid commemoration, complete with brass band, on the landing stage, in April 1955. The Mersey ferries Iris and Daffodil were involved in the Royal Navy raid to put the German naval base out of action on April 23, 1918, hence the thanksgiving service and the ferries receiving the prefix Royal to their names, which are carried by their successors, such as Royal Iris, of 1951, left.

PATIENT

A well-ordered and well-dressed crowd wait in the warm weather for the New Brighton ferry on August 1, 1955, on George's Stage.

OPENING UP

Promenading on the Cruise Liner stage is sadly not an activity permitted today (EU security directive, don't you know). But back in May 1958 there were discussions about letting the public stroll the full length of the stage if no liners were in. On Sunday, May 2, 1958, plenty of people enjoy the sea air on George's Stage, with a Manx steamer moored, left.

OPEN DOOR POLICY

Finally, a year later in May 1959, the public were allowed to
stroll along Princes Landing Stage for the first time since 1939.

OLYMPIC EVENT

When the Mersey was chocker with liners, tug tenders were vital for carrying passengers, mail and baggage to and fro across the river to ships unable to be accommodated at the landing stages. One of the most important tendering occasions was when White Star Line's new flagship RMS Olympic visited for one day on June 1, 1911. In this breath-taking photograph by Gwilym Mills from the top of the also new Royal Liver Building, we see White Star's superliner (then the world's latest largest moving manmade object) making her token visit to her port of registry for a charity public opening. This was a sop to Liverpool as the company had moved its express New York service to Southampton in 1907. The White Star tender Magnetic is seen alongside, between between Olympic's two forward funnels. For reasons we all know, her sister ship Titanic never made a similar planned appointment 10 months later. Picture: Carbonara Co, courtesy Paul Bolger/Mark Chatterton collection.

BREEZING IN

Alexandra Towing Co's famous tug tender Flying Breeze is dwarfed by the Cunard liner RMS Carinthia, finally back alongside the landing stage after being trapped in Gladstone Graving Dock by a ship repairers' strike for five months. She sailed for Quebec and Montreal on May 30, 1961, having missed the first five of that year's round voyages. It didn't bode well, only accelerating the trend of passengers switching to longhaul flights.

GREAT SURVIVOR

The Mersey's last tug tender is the unique twin screw, coal-fired SS Daniel Adamson, built at Tranmere in 1903, currently undergoing restoration to full public working order, in Sandon Dock, Liverpool. Constructed for the Shropshire Union Canal & Railway Co's ferry service from Ellesmere Port to Liverpool, she was sold to become the Manchester Ship Canal directors' inspection vessel and later saved from the scrapyard for £1 by the Daniel Adamson Preservation Society. She's seen at George's Stage in 1947 ready to embark directors and VIPs for a trip to Bridgewater House, Runcorn, for the MSC AGM.

> # "When the Mersey was full of liners, tug tenders were vital for carrying passengers, mail and baggage, across the river."

TENDER SIGHT

The Mersey's largest tender was White Star's 619 gross tons, twin screw, oil-fired SS Magnetic, seen shortly before sale to Alexandra Towing Co, approaching the landing stage in January 1933.

RIVAL RESPONSE

Cunard Line's answer to White Star Line's Olympic and Titanic was RMS Aquitania, dubbed the "Ship Beautiful". Unlike Olympic, Aquitania came alongside the Princes Stage for her maiden voyage to New York, in May 30, 1914. The celebratory send-off was minimal due to the sinking of Canadian Pacific's Empress of Ireland the previous day, inbound from Quebec to Liverpool, with the loss of 1,012 lives. There is a wealth of detail in this remarkable photograph by FA Fyfe, taken from the top of the Royal Liver Building. Note the Manx paddle steamer ahead of Aquitania and the New Brighton Tower (taller than Blackpool Tower), far top right.

MEMORIAL

The Isle of Man Steam Packet's fleet provided sterling service in both world wars as troopships and armed cruisers. Above is Mona's Queen on her maiden voyage from the stage in May, 1934. While on wartime duties in the English Channel in May, 1940, she struck a mine near Dunkirk, on her way with fresh water for troops on the beaches, and sank in two minutes. There were 24 dead, with 17 of them from the Isle of Man. On the 70th anniversary of Mona's Queen's sinking, one of her anchors was raised to form a permanent commemoration at Port St Mary, Isle of Man. Here it is awaiting restoration in January, 2011, at Cammell Laird Shipyard, where the ship was built.

❝ While on wartime duties in the English Channel, Mona's Queen struck a mine near Dunkirk – there were 24 dead. **❞**

UNLUCKY LACONIA

Seen in happier times, is Cunard's RMS Laconia, being waved off on a murky Mersey for a cruise to the West Indies and West Africa, on January 22, 1932, with just 250 passengers including "many well-known personalities". Laconia had made the first proper world cruise in 1922, but unfortunately this was not her main claim to fame. Ten year's later, on September 12, 1942, Laconia carrying some 348 British, 1,800 Italian POWs and 160 Polish guards, was torpedoed by U-156 off west Africa. The U-boat commander, Werner Hartenstein began rescuing survivors with other U-boats. While under Red Cross banners, the U-boats were bombed by a US Liberator aircraft.

This event caused German Navy chief Admiral Doenitz to issue the "Laconia Order" to stop U-boats trying to rescue civilian survivors and ushering in unrestricted submarine warfare. Half of all onboard Laconia lost their lives including Capt Rudolph Sharpe, who had survived Lancastria's sinking.

CHANGING TIMES

Above, demolition of the great Princes Landing Stage continues around Mersey ferry commuters as they cross the gleaming timber decking after an early morning shower, in January, 1974.

FAREWELL VIEW

Visitors to see liners at Princes Landing Stage finally had the viewing platform was roofed over and the front fully glazed, in March, 1956. RMS Saxonia, right, on Cunard's Canadian service demonstrates what the public could see.

BIG LIFT

Floating crane Mersey Mammoth takes the strain in July, 1973, as it removes one of George's Stage's fixing arms which had done stalwart duty for nearly 100 years. The usual appreciative Pier Head audience comes to watch the destruction of a city and port landmark. At least the tug Brocklebank, centre, survives at Mersey Maritime Museum.

FINAL DESTINATION I

Alexandra Tugs haul away a section of George's Stage for scrapping, in November 1973. Cammell Laird shipyard is in the background with a Liverpool pilot boat, back centre.

FINAL DESTINATION II

Left, the dire state of the landing stage is epitomised by the Isle of Man gangway (seen in better state on p44), which had crashed onto the river bed after a storm in December, 1974.

SINKING FEELING

The replacement Irish-built ferry landing stage was a disastrous investment, breaking away and sinking in January, 1976 after a storm which also drove the supertanker Myrina, seen on her way to Anglesey, onto a mudbank off Dingle.

MUCKED UP

After sitting on the riverbed mud for six weeks, the stage was raised and engineers surveyed the wreckage with a view to restoration.

DOWN, DOWN

Matters really came to a head when the Mersey Ferries landing stage once again started to go under due to high tides and gale force winds. Staff were evacuated before the stage started to dip on January 22, 2006. By March 2, 2006, only the circus-style bell tent roof was showing. It helped provide the impetus for properly refurbishing the Pier Head and its landing stages.

SHINE ON

After demolition of the landing stages by 1974, visiting cruise liners once again had to be tendered as they did a century earlier, until Liverpool Cruise Terminal opened in 2008. Here, passengers enjoy the sunshine on a Mersey ferry tendering a visit by Royal Caribbean International's Splendour of the Seas, anchored mid-river.

NOT SO SPLENDID

Conditions can quickly turn nasty on the Mersey as seen in this lower view of the liner. Tendering on the highly changeable Mersey was unpopular with cruise passengers (especially from the US) and cruise lines quickly abandoned Liverpool as a destination on the otherwise expanding round UK cruise business.

GET AWAY

Leaving the snow bedecked-stage to sail for sunnier climes than Douglas, Isle of Man, is Elder Dempster Line's beautiful flagship m/v Aureol, on February 7, 1969. Aureol will call at Las Palmas, Freetown, Monrovia, Tema, Apapa, Lagos and return.

SAFELY HOME

Out of the dense fog from New York on February 6, 1960, came RMS Carinthia, commanded by Capt Geoffrey Marr, after taking five hours to crawl up the river and safely moor at Princes Stage. Note also the gloomy-looking crew with suitcases boarding the Alexandra tug, left, and the VW Beetle puttering along the stage.

ALMOST FAIRYLAND

Back in 1976, on March 27, snow covered both Princes Landing Stage and the Isle of Man Steam Packet's fine turbine steamer King Orry, as recorded by purser John Shepherd.

TERMINAL VELOCITY

Even the latest landing stage built for the £19m Liverpool Cruise Terminal had its snagging problems and delays. Here the one of the Terminal's pontoons with its office gets a final few tweaks at Cammell Laird No 5 dockyard, at Birkenhead, in early August, 2007.

AT LAST

Her big smile says it all. The newly appointed Liverpool Cruise Terminal manager Angie Redhead views with approval the very first arrival at the latest landing stage, Seven Seas Voyager, on August 9, 2007.

RIPPLE EFFECT

Two years later Seven Seas Voyager returned and her mirror image shimmers in the river's ripples, in this fine study by Colin Lane.

ROYAL APPROVAL

The World's most famous ocean liner, Cunard Line flagship RMS Queen Elizabeth 2, inaugurated the Cruise Liner Terminal, on September 22, 2007, when it was officially opened by HRH the Duke of Kent – seen in this superb shot by Jason Roberts, taken from the Royal Liver Building. QE2 is berthed exactly where Aquitania was (p58/9) in 1914. In fact, QE2 usurped Aquitania's title of Cunard's longest serving liner (36 years) when she was retired after 40 years. These were truly two of the much-loved, lucky liners.

"QE2 – the world's most famous ocean liner."

Saga Cruises' Saga Pearl basks in glorious Mediterranean sunshine at Liverpool Cruise Terminal, caught by Gavin Trafford. Ironically, her departure to Cobh was delayed by storms in the southern Irish Sea.

ROYAL SEND-OFF

Fireworks explode above RMS Queen Mary 2, the world's largest ocean liner, prior to departure from Liverpool Cruise Terminal on her maiden visit on October 21, 2009, pictured by photographer Colin Lane.

CENTENARY

Fly Navy 100, the 100th anniversary of the Fleet Air Arm (the Royal Navy's air force) was celebrated in Liverpool, on October 23, 2009, in spectacular style. HMS Illustrious hosted HRH the Duke of York, who took the salute of a fly-past comprising 40 multi-period aircraft in "Balbo" formation – an amazing sight as they converged simultaneously over the carrier for just 40 seconds.

STEALTH WARNING

The forbidding looking new Type 45 air defence destroyer HMS Daring, doyenne of the new D class, on her maiden visit to Liverpool Cruise Terminal on May 22, 2009, just after entering service. Daring's distinctive "stealth" angular profile and pyramidical superstructure reduce her radar signature to that of a small fishing boat.

WIND POWER

The stated desire by Liverpool City Council to open up the Cruise Terminal for community use has been grasped by the newly-formed Merseyside Adventure Sailing Trust. MAST's aim is make Liverpool the tall ship adventure training centre for northern UK. Two of the tall ships most regularly used by MAST are Pelican and Stavros Niarchos (seen right). MAST chairman Jim Graves is seen at the wheel of Pelican, which on September 22, 2012, will undertake the first transatlantic voyage under sail for fare paying passengers from Liverpool in more than 100 years.

STUNNING

Shafts of bright sunshine illuminate Princess Cruises'
Grand Princess, the Liverpool Clipper, from the Round
the World Clipper Yacht Race and a motor cruiser
against a stormy sky, in Colin Lane's masterful study.
Grand Princess is doyenne of her class and at 109,000
gross tons, with 3,100 berths and costing $450m, she
was the largest and most expensive passenger ship
ever built at the time of her launch in 1998.

"Costing $450m, Princess Cruises' Grand Princess is doyenne of her class."

EASY LIVING

Outdoor chess on Cunard Line's new Queen Elizabeth, testing a hammock in the Pirates' Cove play area on Holland America Line's flagship Rotterdam, and a round of crazy golf on Princess Cruises' Crown Princess.

COSTA DEL MERSEY

Taking the plunge into
Neptune's Reef Pool
aboard Crown Princess.
Photo: Andy Teebay

CRUCIAL

Liverpool's goal as a cruise port is to achieve turnaround status with liners once again able to start and end voyages from the city centre. The honour to inaugurate such services for the first time in 40 years falls to Cruise & Maritime Voyages m/v Ocean Countess, in May, 2012, right. After a two year gap, Fred Olsen Cruise Lines will also restart services from the Mersey, in 2013. Like C&MV, Fred Olsen Cruise Lines will switch departures from Langton Dock to Liverpool Cruise Terminal, using its m/v Boudicca. Fleet mates Black Watch and Balmoral (seen below in April 2012) have already used the Terminal while calling in on round Britain cruises, giving passengers a taste of what to expect.

> " Liverpool's development as a cruise port is to achive turnaround status. "

ROARING SUCCESS

Above, a Cunard lion door logo on Ocean Countess
revealing her past as Cunard Countess; passengers
board Ocean Countess from Langton Dock, and a photo
finish for cruise liner Black Watch at the Pier Head.

AU REVOIR ... BUT NOT GOODBYE

The Cunard liner Sylvania, seen from a Wallasey ferryboat as she ties up at the Liverpool landing stage for the last scheduled voyage from the port in November 1966. Cunard only 'suspended services', but never actually restarted them from Liverpool. However, nobody back in 1966 would have dared predict the port's cruise renaissance.

With thanks to: Dan Cross, Stephen Guy, Nigel Hughes, John Langley, Pat Moran, John Shepherd and Stuart Wood. Photography: Eddie Barford, Paul Heaps, Colin Lane, James Maloney, Walter McEvoy, Jason Roberts, Andrew Teebay, Gavin Trafford, Neville Willasey and Richard Williams.